The Odds

Previous Books by Suzanne Cleary

Keeping Time (Carnegie Mellon UP 2002)

Trick Pear (Carnegie Mellon UP 2007)

Beauty Mark (BkMk Press 2013)

Crude Angel (BkMk Press 2018)

The Odds

poems

Suzanne Cleary

NÒY Books™

The New York Quarterly Foundation, Inc.
Beacon, New York

NYQ Books™ is an imprint of The New York Quarterly Foundation, Inc.

The New York Quarterly Foundation, Inc.
P. O. Box 470
Beacon, NY 12508

www.nyq.org

First Edition

Set in New Baskerville

Layout and Design by Raymond P. Hammond

Front Cover Image by istock.com/sankai

Library of Congress Control Number: 2024952947

ISBN: 978-1-63045-113-4

For David

CONTENTS

The odds are we should never have been born.
Not one of us. Not one in 400 trillion to be
exact......
When you think you might be
through with this body and soul, look down
at an anthill or up at the stars, remember
your gambler chances, the bounty
of good luck you were born for.

Dorianne Laux, "Life on Earth"

EMERGENCY ROOM

When it's your heart you go to the front of the line,
ahead of the hump-backed woman holding a rosary
and the construction worker holding his side
and the woman with long brown hair holding a baby.
You go ahead of the boy with his arm in a towel,
his father holding a cellphone and not looking up.
You walk two steps and then you feel a wheelchair
at the back of your knees, and you sit. I sat.
The florescent light seemed to shimmer like a bead
curtain, and I'm not saying that I saw my life flash
before me, but next I was seeing that day in Rome
when I stood inside the front door of my hotel
watching rain, sudden and hard, fall,
and that old man appeared with a blue plastic bucket
full of umbrellas. How happy I was, I remembered,
to have my choice of colors: red, blue, black, yellow.
I chose a red one, then I put it back, I wanted
the yellow. Everyone on our tour was choosing,
and my husband helping me open the cheap
overpriced umbrella, as rain beaded on my glasses
and it became clear that we would let
nothing stop us, not that day.

WORRY STONE

The idea is to carry
in one's pocket
the polished stone

fashioned of pink
marble, with an indentation
the size of a thumb-print:

a place to send tension
out of one's body
into stone, simply

by touching the stone,
stroking it, by turning it over
and over

and over,
until it grows warm
and boring, which is good,

which is as it should be,
one's thoughts turning back
to the larger world,

that contains things
like the house
you once saw

through the bus window
in Utah. It sat at the base
of a rocky mountain

whose name you never
knew, a single-story
stone ranch,

in its front yard
a 30-ton, maybe
40-ton, rock.

How does one weigh
such a thing?
It was tall as the roof.

Someone had placed
a circle of white stones
around the rock,

to make of it
something more,
as you cannot help but do.

Nearly every day
you think of that rock, wonder
what came first,

the rock or the house?
Some days you think
the rock came first.

It made the land cheap,
bought by someone
who believed the worst

had happened,
he would be safe
there, in the dark blue shadow

of the mountain.
Other days you decide
the house came first,

built by someone who believed
that nothing in the world
could harm her, this the woman

you would choose to be:
she who sits in her front window
with a mug of tea

while a 40-ton rock
takes a wild bounce
and flies over the roof.

FOR THE POET WHO WRITES TO ME
WHILE STANDING IN LINE AT CVS, WAITING
FOR HIS MOTHER'S PRESCRIPTION

for Russell Jackson

It's nothing that you flat out say, Russell, but your email
reminds me that six months into pandemic, five months
into quarantine, CVS remains open 24 hours, its harsh
blue-white light steady, as nothing in nature is steady,

those long florescent bulbs still dive-bombing lumens
so that midnight is bright as 8 a.m., or 4 a.m., or 2 p.m.,
or 7:30 p.m. You can see that I struggle to carry
one thought to the next, these long days. I spend hours

on the Internet, becoming expert on the height of actors
from Hollywood's Golden Age, on the 25 Cutest Photos
of four-year-old Princess Charlotte. I now know
that Elizabeth Bishop was a bit taller than I am,

a bit heavier. Her clothes would be too big for me,
as no doubt her shoes. Russell, what is it that supposedly
concentrates the mind wonderfully? Samuel Johnson said it,
in Boswell's biography, which I have never read and never

will. I know my limits. Lately, I think that I know little else
worth knowing. My only advice for your poems, Russell:
wash your hands for as long as it takes to sing Happy Birthday.
Did you know that song is no longer copyrighted? Five years ago,

U. S. District Court Judge George H. King ruled
Happy Birthday is public domain, the 1935 patent applied
only to the melody and specific arrangements of the tune,
but not to the actual song itself. When Judge King writes

17

actual song, he means lyrics, but I hear him saying
song is something beyond the reach of law, beyond reach
of language. Song is like a kernel of light, inside of things,
steady. Russell, be like CVS. I don't know what this means,

be like CVS. Russell, dare to say what doesn't make sense,
then wait patiently to see the sense inside of it. Be like CVS.
Be like the bewildering variety of toothpastes, decongestants,
hair conditioners. Be like orange Velcro knee braces,

like spools of pastel ribbon that hums, pulled across a scissor.
Be like the aisle of bare shelves where the cleaning products stood,
where the white metal shelves now display only how each shelf,
with a simple ingenious hook, fits into the frame.

I'm telling you nothing that you don't already know, Russell.
Be like whatever accepts the horrid light, and shines in it.
Be like the 8-ounce can of lightly salted cashews, for which
you are newly willing to pay $12.99, as you stand in line

waiting for the blue-gloved hands to hold out to you
the small white bag, which is not for you,
except in that you are the one
who will carry it where it must go.

BUMPER STICKER

for CB

This is for Anna, the minister's wife, who says, *Hell, no!* No way
will she let the church secretary affix a bumper sticker to her car:
the fish symbol that stands for Christian, but which looks

like a doodle drawn while the mind is elsewhere, or like an editor's
mark, yes, crossing out what becomes invisible beneath.
No way does Anna want her driving to reflect on her faith: distracted,

impatient, often unsuited to the conditions, except when she drives
that stretch where her youngest daughter 16, crashed that rainy
    night.
It was October, the maples gold and red, leaves not ready

to fall, falling after the daylong pour, which in truth was light,
just mist as Julia drove home, everything shining.
No one is safe on that road built when cars were small and slow,

when trees now crowding the shoulder, their limbs overhanging,
were saplings, planted not by gardeners but by wind carrying seeds
through the air and then dropping them. We understand some
    things:

the air drops a seed, a bird eats the seed, the bird flies away.
The bird shits out the seed, which takes root. A tree grows.
A car hits the tree. The car is totaled. The girl lives, or not.

This time, the girl lives. Julia lives. Praise God, if so inclined,
even briefly inclined, as something flies close—something
swift and light and then gone, barely seen as it passes.

LOVESPOON

The idea is to take a single piece of wood
        and carve it into a spoon, present it
to your beloved as a proposal of marriage,

the handle thick with hearts and doves
        and bells and horseshoes and, because
this spoon originates in the North Atlantic,

with cables and braids and knots, as on Aran
        sweaters knit to protect the sailor
from cold and, to speak the hard truth of it,

to identify the body washed ashore.
        The spoon's handle roils with ornament
that emerges in the working, one shape morphing

into another, or into a nameless shape
        between definite shapes.
The carver does not belabor the distinction

between figure and ground,
        as love does not belabor the distinction
between chore and gift,

but when it is time
        to fashion the spoon's bowl,
accuracy and proportion must reign:

the bowl substantial yet graceful,
        neither too wide nor too deep.
Although the lovespoon most often

gleams from the mantle or hangs
         from a decorative hook,
it must be able to serve

stewed carrots to a baby,
         strained soup to a parent.
It is made for use, as love may teach us

to take the deep bowl of each day
         by whatever rough handle,
and lift the limewood to our lips.

AGAIN, I HEAR MYSELF LECTURING MY STUDENTS ON A SUBJECT ABOUT WHICH I KNOW VERY LITTLE

We read aloud together *I heard a fly buzz,*
and then we do it again, so as to feel the poem in our bodies.
Then the room, no surprise, goes silent, until Michelle

says that slam audiences praise the poet
by snapping their fingers. She snaps, snaps again.
Then Joseph snaps, then Kim, even the quiet students

who seldom look up, and I, too, add my lame finger-snap.
Then we hear it: my voice saying *La Scala,*
and none of us knows what will come next,

for I know as little about Milan's opera house
as I know of Euclidean geometry,
for that matter, of Euclid, whom I always confuse

with the one who sat in the bath, noting that the size
of his body related somehow to the rise of water
as he sank into a stone tub.

Does anyone know what La Scala is? I ask,
for it is polite to ask, though I know it unlikely
that anyone in this class knows. No one knows.

*It's an opera house in Milan, Italy. It's famous
for its rude audiences,* which is the hook
that keeps my students from checking their cellphones,

from doodling in the margins of their rented textbooks.
When the audience at La Scala does not like a singer,
they boo. They throw things onto the stage.

What do they throw? Milo shouts. *They throw fruit,*
I inform him. *They throw tomatoes they had been saving*
for their best spaghetti sauce. Imagine it, I add,

women in white elbow-length gloves
throwing tomatoes, men in diamond cufflinks
throwing tomatoes, throwing green peppers.

I tell my students one thing that I know to be true
of La Scala: some singers refuse to sing there,
unwilling to make themselves a target,

willing to forego possible triumph
in order to avoid humiliation,
and my students now are silent—

the one who cares for her drug-addicted mother,
the one who writes of the basketball court
where he buys new underwear from the trunk of a car.

I speak softly. *Don't let anyone,*
I begin, not knowing where I am headed.
Don't let anyone tell you that you are less

than someone who goes to the opera,
or tell you that you will not travel the world,
but I can hear my words falling flat. I am failing

to hit the right notes of this aria
in the florescent-lit opera house of Third Floor East,
Academic II, where my students already know

that life is an opera, know that an opera's plot
seldom makes sense, that the way to survive an opera
is to give yourself over to it, to sink deeply in,

or to let yourself float on the sparkling surface, drifting
to some place that you cannot yet name,
as did that man in the tub, yes, Archimedes!

If we had more time, I would tell my students
his story, for while he is most famous
for, at his moment of insight, shouting

Eureka!, Archimedes spent most of his time
in quiet calculation, alone with his questions,
scratching charcoal upon stone to design catapults

for hurling boulders into the Roman army,
so as to defend his city from marauders, each motley one
wondering how in the world they ended up here.

TO THE PERSON AT THE ZOOM POETRY READING, UNMUTED, DOING HAND LAUNDRY

June 6, 2020

I hear you. Meaning not only that I hear water
circle and splash, the burp and swish of hands
lowering and raising fabric

at a sink within earshot of your computer.
I mean that I hear you. I hear your need
to stand and do something useful

on this spring afternoon thousands march
through the streets to protest the brutality,
the racism, upon which this country was built,

and builds. After months of quarantine,
people sweating into their homemade masks
stand shoulder to shoulder.

Two blocks from here, my neighbors stand
in a park, all of them, I think, my street quiet,
my house silent except for these poems, read

from rooms that fit only partially
into the Zoom boxes. We are four poets,
and maybe fifty others, leaning slightly forward

to listen. We all hear you, I think.
I hear your need to rise, to turn a spigot
and make something clean.

One hundred years ago, hand laundry
was called *smalls*: slips and baby dresses,
anything with even a sprig of embroidery.

After washing the smalls—I think
there was no singular *small*—you'd place
each one between towels, press to remove

most of the water, then hang it to dry.
Truth be told, the sound of water
is not poor soundtrack for a poetry reading,

for the sound of water is the sound
of time, of suspension and transport.
Water is the source of life.

Still, I wish you had pressed Mute
like the countless others who listened,
their hands open and soft under the water,

their sleeves pushed up,
as for the other work
we all must do together.

I THINK THAT I'VE FIGURED IT ALL OUT

after "In the Land of Fragrance," by Colleen Creamer,
The New York Times, August 13, 2017

I think that I've figured it all out: we're all living downwind
from the glove factory, downwind from the ash and the alum
that supple the skin of the deer and the cow and the goat until the skin
is hairless, slick as spun silk, smooth as a doe's ear, and ready
for stretching and drying and dyeing, then cut into shape, then one shape lain
across its twin, then tacked and sewn together with stitches so fine they cannot
be seen, can only be felt by the fingertips of the women who work in the
    dim room
for room-and-board, work upwind from us and the fields that surround us
thickly planted with rose, with jasmine, with lavender, thin petals brutal
    with scent,
fields divided and sown so the air will be so fragrant, so that we will be so
    soshed
with scent that we struggle to breathe, struggle to think of the factory just
    over the hill,
and of the other people, too, those who struggle to choose between navy
    and cordovan,
between ivory and butter-yellow, and then they choose both, and then they
    ask the girl
if she can remove the tiny bone button at the wrist and replace it with pearl.

GLOVE

It was a cheap glove, green cotton,
the kind that hangs on a wire rack
at a truck stop, a glove

for checking oil or pumping gas,
for unloading crates when you get
to wherever you've been driving

ten hours, not a glove
for Manhattan, the midtown branch
of the New York Public Library,

although it was always cold
in the basement stacks,
where books waited on long tables

for one of us Class 3 workers
to sort them onto carts.
Billy and I would wheel the books

to their proper aisle, return each
to its place. Down there, in bedrock,
as each subway train passed

the metal shelves shuddered,
books trembling as our hands
trembled, cold even in summer,

this summer the last summer
of the brass subway tokens,
which still worked

in the new turnstiles
installed for the shiny gold chips
with higher fare.

I would stand at the book cart,
choosing the books, handing them
one by one to Billy, who sat on the floor,

then knelt, then, finally,
he stood beside me, so close
in those narrow book-spined aisles

I could smell the faint scent
of Lifebuoy soap, and sandalwood,
I think. We always agreed

to take our break together,
which meant ten minutes
in a room beside the boiler,

where we each had a locker.
I would lift from its hook
the dark green cashmere sweater

I had found in a thrift shop.
On the shoulder, where
one would pin a corsage,

there was a flower of tiny pearls
that pleased me each time I saw it.
One day, as we sat

in the orange chairs
by the soda machine, Billy told me
that for the past three months

he had been getting up early
to catch the first train of the day.
He'd stop at each token booth

on the line, to buy tokens
in bulk, as many as one person
was allowed to buy. He'd ride

to the end of the line, then
back to midtown by eight.
He did the same after work:

home, by way of Far Rockaway.
He would have enough tokens,
he told me, to last to the end

of the year, and maybe beyond.
Most of those days felt, to me,
like the same day, but another day

also stands out: late afternoon,
across our emptied cart
we stared at each other, knowing

that we had until five o'clock
to do nothing, or anything.
No one would know.

A train idled in the station.
Billy slid from his back pocket
a pair of gloves. He took one, and,

as if he were a mother or father,
he held the glove
open for my hand.

It is pale green,
a gardening glove,
thin elastic at the wrist.

Does it matter to this poem
that Billy is black?
Does it not matter

that I am white?
Who can say? Who will say?
Why and how does it matter

that at this moment—
I mean not this moment
in the library basement,

but this moment in the poem—
I turn away from the glove,
as I did on that day?

IT IS SAID

after *La Bella Lingua*, by Dianne Hales

It is said that until 1950
every Italian could recite by heart
twenty-five lines of Dante,

so that in 1944
the partisan shepherd
stationed at Pisa, ordered to shoot

anyone out after dark without ID,
would ask the stranger
to recite from *The Divine Comedy*

in order to prove himself Italian,
the dialect to prove himself local.
It is said that one night

the footsteps were a professor
of literature, the text the *Inferno*,
seventeenth canto: the one where the usurers

sit in the sand,
unable to lift their eyes
from purses hanging from their necks.

The professor's frozen breath
sparkled, rising from the wooden-shack
check-point, the professor helpless

but to love these words,
which make music
of wretchedness,

the shepherd helpless
but to close his eyes,
whether from emotion or fatigue

it would be hard to say.
It is said that, at line 117,
the professor halted.

Silent, he raised his hands
to his mouth, as if fingertips
could lift the words from his lips.

The shepherd opened his eyes,
waited. Then he cleared his throat,
recited the rest of the canto.

This is the meaning of *every*:
the shepherd in torn smock
as well as the man in frayed necktie,

as well as no need for others
to remark upon the transition
from one voice to the other,

smooth as when a woman
with a basket of potatoes
passes the braided handle

from one arm
to the other arm,
so as to carry it home.

I GO BACK, AS I AM TODAY

I go back. I go back as I am today to 8th grade,
a Friday in late April, 8th period, last class of the day, English:
Mr. Winslow standing with his back to us as he looks out the window
at a long hedge aflare with forsythia, its unmutable golden shiver.

His arms hang heavy. Then he turns, looks at each of us, one
    at a time.
I go back as I am today to the small desk where I still fit comfortably,
but today I know how young we all are, including our teacher
who is balding, his ruddy forehead deeply lined.

Today I know what our teacher is about to say: William,
who is absent today, whose desk is the last in the row by the window,
last night William shot himself, with his father's gun, in a barn.
I go back to Mr. Winslow wondering aloud if he was wrong

to have had us read Edwin Arlington Robinson's "Richard Corey."
Implacable are the forsythia. Their color matches that of the
    school buses
slowly arriving, waiting to take us home. Each year the forsythia
will return for each of us. As I am today, I know this.

I go back as I am today and I see for the first time the bravery
of doubt, of displaying doubt to others. I discover the girl who I was
still lives inside of me. I go back to that moment I heard the word
barn. I smell hay. I hear chickens squawking as they wait to be fed.

REUNION

By the time of your 40th high school reunion,
      there are old people who are younger
            than you are, and you understand

soon you always will walk at the pace
      of this group tour of your alma mater
            or mine, where fifteen of us take turns

staring into the locked chemistry lab
      and ducking into the cafeteria.
            Our guide is an honors student

who gets extra credit for leading us
      on this bright Saturday afternoon,
            who maneuvers us up the short staircase

into East Hall, where she pauses,
      perhaps so that we can catch our breath,
            perhaps to command our full attention

as she reminds us of the location
      of tonight's dinner downtown. We are,
            I see, within sight of the room

where I fell in love with poetry,
      senior year, last semester, a class
            I took purely because it fit

into my schedule. Is there time enough
      to see that room? I ask, and I receive.
            Our guide steps politely to the side

as she opens the door.
      The room is predictably smaller,
            and yet smaller still: divided in two

by a new wall, which has stood there,
     probably, for decades.
          There is a door in that wall, open

to a room that was part
     of the original room, but I enter
          neither. No one, I notice,

feels the need to enter—
     a moment of awkwardness
          I choose to find beautiful.

From the doorway I can see
     where I sat as Mr. Lisowski opened
          Robert Bly's *Silence in the Snowy Fields*

for what would be the last time
     in my entire long life
          I would begin listening to a poem

without half-holding my breath,
     so as better to hear.
          The edge of the deep blue book

rested lightly on the table
     as the walls of the room dissolved,
          I guess, for I saw the walls

reassemble as the end-of-class bell rang.
     There they were: the pale blue walls,
          and the possibility that this color

is like eggs in a nest, or like
     my grandmother's hair.
          There was now another room

inside of that room,
     and inside of everything
          that I would ever see.

CAHOOTS

I figured it was somewhere up near Albany, maybe a suburb
where the governor lived, but what did I know?
I was a kid, I didn't drive, and how far can you pedal

on a banana-style seat, with playing cards clothes-pinned
to the back wheel? Every week someone else
was in Cahoots, had traveled to that famous town.

I wondered, what was the draw of Cahoots
for the mechanics who charged my father twice
for the wipers on our Limekist Green station wagon?

What was the draw for the freckled twins
who smashed our pumpkin, for the blue-haired sisters
who cheated at church Bingo? This much I knew:

in Cahoots people played Bingo, although I could not say
if there were churches up there. And I knew this: no one
was ever alone. There were always at least two in Cahoots.

No one who had seen it ever spoke of it,
the stories of Cahoots left for others to tell, my grandfather,
especially, who knew of more people in Cahoots

than did anyone else for miles. He named names.
He named neighborhoods where, for example,
no one would speak Slovak to him,

where Slovaks would not speak their own
language. *They're all in Cahoots*, he would tell me
in a tone that suggested overcrowding, a place

I would not want to live, or even to visit. Better to stay
in my hometown, with my mother and father,
in our modest but pleasant split-level.

Never fond of travel, each July we inexplicably packed
the wagon for our week at the Jersey shore. One year,
a horseshoe crab, like a crusty hubcap laced with green

slime, washed onto the sand. My father and two boys
slipped driftwood under the crab, nudged it
onto the lip of rising tide, which lifted it, carried it

beyond sight. Already I knew that, somehow,
the waves and the moon were in cahoots.
I knew that each day was shorter than the day before.

If that summer I suspected that cahoots was not a place,
I was wrong, too young to know that we all
end up in cahoots, whether a penthouse downtown

or a ranch in Cahoots County.
I was still so young that I'd have sworn cross-my-heart
I would never be in cahoots, not ever, not me.

THERE IS SO SUCH THING AS A STUPID QUESTION

I ask myself, When did I first hear
there is no such thing as a stupid question?
but I am stupid to ask, for it must have been

middle school, each of us starting
to see ourselves as others might see us,
growing too self-conscious to admit that, yes,

we had questions, we did not understand
long division, nor its vile cousin the percentage.
We had grown unaccountably afraid to ask

how the egg found its way to the fallopian tube,
nor why it's always called *your period*, singular,
which had led one of us to believe

that it would happen only once.
Our teacher must have promised us
there is no such thing as a dumb question

thinking this was her last chance to do so,
for she could see that we were starting to doubt
the intelligence of adults. There was a war.

There were police officers lining Court Street
while a crowd chanted for justice. What is justice?
Why are some people certain of everything,

and others of nothing? What are the odds
these groups ever will speak civilly to each other?
For forty years I have believed in the sovereignty

of the question, that the stupid question does not exist,
forty years until this evening, when *Hi, Neighbor!*,
a website for paranoid locals, posts

Is it OK to eat the sticker that the grocery store
sticks onto the fruit? My neighbor continues,
I'm worried about my children,

and I share her worry. But do I share her worry?
What percentage of me feels connection
to this woman with three children under the age of five,

who probably stood beside me in Stop 'n Shop,
weighing an avocado in her palm
against the coins in her pocket?

DIVISION

When I walk up the long sweep of Division Street
        that connects Center City to Mortgage Hill,
            sometimes my body remembers

walking from the first metro stop in Montmartre, up
        to the corner of that street of cafes
            where the sidewalk was crowded with artists

balancing on three-legged stools, drawing portraits
        of tourists as other tourists passed, as couples
            decided, inconveniently, to walk arm-in-arm,

all of this so vivid today, as if something inside of me
        still climbs that morning, 30 years ago.
            I had woken with my period, dull

cramp like a thumbprint of heat in my side, the knot
        less pain than knowledge, less knowledge than
            the idea of knowledge, which was nothing

to stop me from eating my croissant with milky coffee,
        then heading to the street where great artists had lived.
            Apparently, and probably since the beginning of time,

anyone can call themselves an artist,
        which is likely more good than bad, but I remember
            standing at the edge of that sidewalk unimpressed,

although by then it was noon, when artists prefer not to work
        because the sun is directly overhead: no shadows
            to sharpen edges, to help define form.

Each stood a pad of paper on their knees
        and leaned back, as if remembering the art teacher
                saying, *Draw with your whole body!*

and so they each drew with the entire arm, long
        swift charcoal lines. They would stop and stare, use
                the side of a fist to wipe away stray ash

or the line itself, although a shadow of each mark
        would remain, a vibration beneath the later, better line,
                a map of the journey toward seeing.

I wiped sweat from my forehead.
        Someone offered me a chair I refused.
                I don't know what I was looking for,

but when each artist had finished
        and turned the pad toward the model, I saw this:
                however bad the portrait,

the model smiled and nodded,
        convinced the likeness remarkable.
                It would be years before I understood that,

whatever we look at, we see ourselves,
        and years later before I understood that the body
                is the least of who we are, of what carries me

up this hill, my arms swinging, lifting my body
        into a rhythm that seems part of everything I can see
                or have seen, have forgotten and remember again.

BRIEF GUIDE

What was I thinking when I bought *A Brief Guide*
to the Great Philosophers, other than, well, it's brief?
What was I thinking when I thought I would read

a history of the French Revolution in French, or,
for that matter, in English? What did I need to know
about Gregorian chant or the mammals of North America?

What did I need to know, beyond how Gustav Stickley
constructed a chair: dovetailing each joint, no nails needed,
the chair's strength and stability due to the weight of the wood.

LIFE CLASS

To force his students to see
      the model, instead of their drawings
            of the model, Eakins bans pencil and paper

from the room where the nude man stands, beside
      the gas lamp suspended to draw shadows
            from the body's angles and curves,

each darkness suggesting the armature
      upon which the shapes depend.
            All is silent, still, a full

ten minutes until Eakins rings a glass bell,
      students run to the door, press messily out.
            They climb the staircase two steps

at a time, toward the room where easels stand ready.
      Three flights they must climb, carrying
            the image of the model in their heads,

where it flickers and fades, comes again into focus.
      The first lesson: to see. The second lesson
            a distant second: to turn it into something else.

IN MEMORY OF THE FORGOTTEN

after Peter Robb's M: The Man Who Became Caravaggio

In Rome in 1600 several famous painters now forgotten
shared a pair of linen wings tall as young poplars,
their ivory fabric grayed, frayed from leaning against
whatever props had collected in whatever small studio,

these two wings joined with rope and a harness
so the model could strap himself into the wings,
dangle above the head of the painter,
stare lovingly down into Christ's face

and likewise into the other faces of the poor
who posed for the price of a piece of bread, a cup of wine,
likewise into the face of this painter who needed an angel,
and fast, to satisfy the eye of the Inquisition, which could be

anywhere, and therefore was here in this very room,
where imagination lived, and held its breath.

XAVIER, GET OUT OF THAT TREE!

Xavier, get out of that tree!
Xavier, your name rises up from the river,
from some narrow window

muscled open, someone leaning out,
Xavier! your name drifting uphill,
toward our town with its one grocery,

in its window a sign *Mask Required,*
a smaller sign *Food Stamps Accepted Here.*
Xavier, is it already time for lunch?

Are you being called in for tomato soup,
or is someone afraid that you might fall
from your favorite place?

You sit at the top of the tallest red maple,
skinny rump perched on the last branch
that will hold your weight.

Can you see the boy two houses away,
who plays with the dog he named Fire?
Can you see his sister reading in her room?

Can you see the Hudson River clear
to its far shore, how it reflects the first
rusty leaves, blue shallows shining

like a tin can with its lid peeled back?
If you look north, can you see the spot
where the river first flows free

of the ocean, where the salt water
that drifts far upstream finally relents,
leaves the river to itself: salt-free, cold?

Xavier, when you hear your name,
do you consider sliding your rump
to a lower branch in order to climb down,

or to see from a new angle?
Do you see the men in work boots
on the gravel road by the river?

Do you see the pickup truck stop,
the men climb up? Can you see the blue
baseball cap, fallen from a back pocket?

And the post office, the police station
with its fleet of white cars,
its van with bars on the windows,

can you see them from your tree?
Can you see as far as the hospital,
masked orderlies lying in the grass

beside the sign *Emergency*?
Do you see them remove their masks
to eat? Behind them,

do you see the glass door
slide open, the baby in stroller
pump its arms in the cool air?

Xavier, closer, can you see
who cups her hands to her mouth
to call you down from this place

where you would live forever?
Can you see her looking up,
her eyes closed, calling?

MURAL

for Karen Allen

I never asked City Hall for permission.
They didn't see it until it was done,
too late for anyone to say no,
Karen tells me as we walk from the plaza,
crossing four streets and two parking lots,
the alley behind the laundromat.

It's late October, the last warm night
of the year, we figure, our coats falling open.
It's still light at seven, although lit mostly
from the half moon, from the strings of cheap
white Christmas lights the shops hang year-round:
the bakery, the florist, the shoe repair

with its window of wooden feet
that have outpaced their usefulness
except as reminders of the shoemaker's father
and grandfather. There are pale blue lights
circling the window of the Mexican restaurant
that stayed open throughout the pandemic,

its foil pans steaming in the shivering air.
We are close to the mural before we can see it,
on the back wall of the Empire Beauty School,
facing the clinic where doctors treat
anyone who enters. Even before I see it
I am wondering how I had forgotten

the beauty of my poor city, those months
my heartbeat raced then stuttered. How had I
forgotten the people who are out this evening,
pouring from buildings where they work
second shift? This is their break. This is when
the man who mops the bank's marble floor

leans against the drop deposit as if he owns it,
when the woman who owns the used book shop
shutters the green bin of free books,
in case of rain. While I sat in my chair all night
and all day, taking small white pills and trying
to sleep, then trying to be awake,

Karen found graph paper, sketched the mural.
She entered the beauty school and introduced herself,
got the owner's permission to paint the wall,
a 12 by 60 foot mural completed in one week.
She worked beside family and friends, beside strangers
who had stopped to watch, then took a brush

and did as she said: create unnameable shapes,
for the mural is abstract, long arching strokes
of peach-pink and sand-blue, pistachio, white tea.
It is a vision of spring's muscular interior,
the origin of leaf and blossom. It is what
we cannot see of spring, beyond our sight.

THE BEAUTY

for Gabrielle Freeman

She called it *the beauty*
        and saw it nearly every day

from her attic studio, the snake
        sunning itself on top of the stone wall,

all near-six-feet of it shining like black oil,
        like a slice of midnight come early

then gone, woven back into summer's grasses.
        But she knew it stayed near,

so the morning she carried her pail to the barn
        and found the nests empty,

hens squawking and eggs gone,
        she knew it was time

to take beauty into her own hands,
        although this proved more a matter

of holding open the empty feed sack
        while beauty, untouched, poured itself in.

Biting one end of a rope, she tied the sack tight,
        dragged it to her truck, settled it

onto the floor beneath the glove compartment.
        How far did she need to drive? Who knew?

Edge of the Blue Ridge she released it,
       folded the empty sack over her arms.

Some days she had seen it in the morning,
       other days late afternoon, unpredictable

the beauty that sometimes one sees
       and sometimes disappears for weeks,

invisible, though it spread itself long and shining
       in clear sight, hungry.

INSIDE THE NEST

The truth is it sickened me,
    what I saw inside the nest:
        the mound of gray down

like a mohair blanket
    tossed into the air
        and let fall,

its corners tucked loosely under
    to fit the nest
        narrow but deep,

the bluish mound
    shivering as a pond shivers
        beneath wind,

breaths shallow breaths
    like a sleeping dog, its stomach
        taupe under sparse hair.

Five birds I saw,
    pressed close to each other
        as if one,

the crown of each head
    the size of a thumbprint
        and too heavy to lift.

Sick rose in my throat as I saw
    what there is before there is
        feather or wing,

when everything is soft and pulsing.
        Better to look away, I thought.
            Better to imagine.

Better to imagine the day
        each bird can lift its head,
            open its hard yellow beak,

take food dropped into that darkness
        where song grows
            if it grows at all.

AGNES MARTIN, I WANT YOUR DRESS

I want it. I want the dress you wore
on those rare occasions when you agreed
to appear at a gallery with your paintings,

those years-long series of square canvases, each
a new note on your scale of pale grids
that people insisted looked like handkerchiefs

or bedsheets hung on a clothesline, despite
your insistence that they were no such thing,
that your paintings referred to nothing

beyond themselves, or, perhaps, each one
a map of the canvas itself, of uninhabited space,
though you rarely deigned to speak of them,

nor to approach and stand beside them, knowing
what was expected of you: that you smile
in black silk tunic, with maybe a single silver pin.

What would I not give to have seen you
in this dress that your biographers mention
only in passing, your orange velvet dress?

I have had to imagine for myself the full skirt,
floor-length, the dropped waist and wide sleeves
so generous that you might have worn,

underneath, your customary attire:
overalls, the linen smock you'd pull off
as the Taos sun rose above the studio

where you worked day and night,
no difference for you between day and night
except when you'd lift your canvas, carry it

to follow the sun. This was your uniform,
well suited to sitting cross-legged on the floor,
then kneeling, then standing, leaning close

as your ballpoint pen drew a straight line
that spanned the canvas, then another line
parallel to that, then another, driven

by something inside of you that never bent
to those claiming your imagery domestic
or portal to the spiritual realm so fashionable

at that time. You worked in art's margins,
at home in the spell cast by rigor, by surrender,
a spell cast over me by your austere vision

and no less by the idea of your orange velvet
dress: heavy, plush, garish, outrageously
present, eternally smelling of primer.

SOPHIA LOREN REVEALS HER SECRET TO STAYING YOUNG

When I get out of a car
or I stand up from a chair,
I never say "Uuhhh."

She pauses
for the camera,
shrugs, laughs.

She wears
the heavy black eyeglasses
worn by Marcello Mastrioanni,

except with orange-red lipstick,
her smile a discipline become habit,
a habit become pleasure.

Walking, she leans slightly
on each arm offered—
to do otherwise

would be ingratitude,
and foolishness at her age,
which she does not deny.

How could she?
There are photographs
of her and her mother in 1948,

feeding soldiers at small tables
in the front room
of her grandmother's house

in Pozzouli, what remained

after the bombs of war.
                    The scar on her chin:

from diving to the floor.
            *Some mornings you don't feel
                    you would like*

to get out of bed, she says,
            but you do.

THE WAR

after Peter Dreher

Leaving the apartment where he'd spent the war,
he saw the water glass beside the sink

and turned back, filled it,
drank, took it,

having seen his future:
to begin each day

with a new painting of the glass,
one day full of water, the next day less, then less,

his future spent, as necessary, refilling
this cheap transportable world,

breakable but never broken,
never drunk from again

except by the air,
which has no end of thirst.

HERMINA

If you had worn three skirts over your nightgown
        and a shirt over that, and a black wool vest, red shawl,
then knotted the blue-with-pink cabbage-rose babushka

under your pointed little chin, and thus you wore for
        the journey every article of clothing to your name,
who could blame you for using your first paycheck

for a store-bought tissue-paper sewing pattern
        for the simple dress you would wear for sixty years:
short-sleeves, round collar, buttons to the waist,

the calf-length skirt slightly gathered, clasped at the waist
        with hook-and-eye, finished with loops for a belt
of the same fabric. Hermina would tie the belt, to save

the expense of a buckle, her waistline growing and shrinking
        and growing, finally narrow as a girl's, and her closet
full of that one dress in navy with polka dots, red with polka dots,

dark green with yellow roses, gray with pink sailboats,
        and Hermina blind but remembering every dress,
and that bank teller who refused to say her strange name.

BASEBALL

for Yehoshua November

Even when young
he could not hit
and could not field.

It was against his nature
to throw a ball at a man.
But, 70 years old, finally

he discovers his place
in the Great American
Pastime. As his wife

scolds, then cautions,
*Do you know how old
you are?* he lowers himself

onto the floor
to sit cross-legged
with his grandsons,

baseball cards spread
in an arc before them.
For the younger boy, he reads

each player's name, card by card.
For the older boy, he listens,
widening his eyes and nodding

as the boy recites statistics,
explains elaborate permutations
of elaborate rules.

And when the boys ask him,
then beg him, he takes
a single card. He holds it close

then far. He stares into the athlete's
young eyes, set in a face aged
prematurely by sun. Then, in keeping

with the game of baseball, slowly
he takes the pen from his jacket,
writes the player's name

across the corner of the card
as if it is the man's autograph.
This man is not Mantle,

nor DiMaggio, those cards framed
and hung on a bedroom wall.
This man is one of the rookies, or

the mid-career player of middling career,
the new card still smelling of fresh
cardboard and stale bubblegum.

In the slant light before prayers,
before dinner, methodically
he signs each card

the boys hand to him,
until the boys grow tired
of their treasured cards,

preferring their grandfather's
knowledge of the inner life
of baseball, stories beginning,

This man writes big
because his eyes are weak
from staring too long at the sun.

This man writes tiny, so that
he can sign his name many times
before his pen runs out of ink.

WHAT YOU GET

after "Boaty McBoatface: What You Get When You Let the Internet Decide," Katie Rogers, *New York Times*, March 21, 2016

A British government agency lets the Internet
name the 287-million-dollar polar research ship,
and someone proposes *Boaty McBoatface*.

Someone seconds the name, someone thirds it, and anyone
can see where this ship is heading: a tidal wave of votes
for *Boaty McBoatface*, a rip current, a tsunami,

thousands of people bobbing, gasping with laughter,
each surprised to discover that they had been waiting
for something to lift them, to lift them together,

as does this name submitted by James Hand,
Public Relations Professional, a title nonexistent
in the fourteenth century, when a messenger

for Pope Benedict XI traveled to Florence, seeking bids
for a papal commission, for a painting for the Vatican.
Asked for his bid, Giotto surveyed his studio.

He chose a blank canvas, dipped a brush in red paint,
drew a perfect circle. The messenger carried it
to the Pope, and who cannot see where this ship

is heading? Giotto gets the commission.
This is what you get. This is what you get
if you are Giotto. But if you are a government agency

whose power is great but subject to approval,
a bottle of champagne will eventually bonk
the polar research ship to pronounce it

The Sir David Attenborough, after the broadcaster
and natural historian, a beloved national treasure,
although this appellation always embarrassed him.

CUPID

Ever since an X-ray of *Girl Reading a Letter at an Open Window* was made more than 40 years ago, scholars have been aware of the Cupid, who stares out of a painting within the painting....But they had always assumed that Vermeer erased the god himself.

"A Vermeer Restoration Reveals a God of Desire,"
New York Times, September 9, 2021

Add this to the list of things we must accept:
that Vermeer hung a poor painting of Cupid
in the famous room where the girl reads a letter,

whether the Cupid a lapse of taste, or a joke,
or an artist's need to make art carry more
than it can plausibly bear.

And if he reconsidered his decision,
if he paused to live for a while
with Cupid, too, reading the letter,

we must accept that Vermeer chose
to let Cupid remain, for it was the hand
of someone else who painted over

the God of Love, regarding him
as an embarrassment or redundancy
in the tenderness of that room

Vermeer had arranged
at the front of his home,
on the second floor

so he could ignore all of Delft
while letting its light caress
the dark table, the fruit, the pitcher

63

seen in many of his paintings,
objects that serve as places
on which to hang one's attention

and thus fall briefly in love.
Here, that light tints the paper
faint blue in the girl's hands

as she reads what critics presume
is a love letter, given the glow
that kisses her forehead.

The same glow touches Cupid,
who has the body of a bulldog
and face of Charlemagne.

How far into tenderness
must Vermeer have traveled
to touch Cupid with such light,

how far into the hideous
that even an observer can see
what lies beneath art's blind labor?

DEFINITION

for David

Drawing is love.
                    Roz Stendhal

Drawing is love is to say *Attention is love,*
but to say it better, with the image

of juicy black ink tracing a contour
of cheek or thigh or pear or cup,

with the image of a stick of charcoal
depositing ash on rough newsprint,

which is to say that Stendhal draws me
to thought of your hand, your soft

square palm, your fingertips lifting my chin
as if you were a painter who studies my face

and my neck, and their relation, so as to see
the essential lines, before the work begins.

WHO AMONG US

What the bulldog lacks in grace
        it makes up for with lack of grace,
thick-set, low-slung, little pig feet shuffling
        through wet red leaves beside the river

as two men follow at some distance,
        brothers, one talking and one nodding,
all three of them swathed in the fog
        of early morning after a night of rain,

the last drops still falling
        from the few leaves remaining.
November is a hard month, swelling
        with darkness and chill, but October

also was hard, despite purple cone flowers
        and goldenrod fizzing with bees.
The one man slowly shakes his head
        and the other man nods,

as if they are in a library or streetcar
        or anywhere, while the dog
noses the fragrant ground, waddles on,
        his one gnarled expression

expressing nothing, even as his hind leg
        slips, and of course the other one follows,
and then the dog is spinning on its stomach
        down the steep bank into the River Wye.

Who among us has not fallen into the River Wye,
        or into its happier tributary, the Wye Not?
Who among us has not tensed at the first signs
        of the trajectory, before

giving in? Dan—this is the dog's name—
        Dan labors to breathe as he burbles
 in the shallows, and then,
        as the record states, *regains the shore,*

all of which can be heard in Edward Elgar's
        Enigma Variations, Opus 36,
the opening bars of Variation II.
        Good boy, Dan. Good boy.

IS IT NORMAL?

Is it normal to watch TV all night,
say, the Fourth of July Weekend marathon of *Your New RV*?
Is it normal to watch with such absorption that you don't snack
or drink, that you talk out loud to the people who inspect RV

after RV? Mostly they are couples and young families,
first swiping fingertips across slick aluminum siding,
noting awnings and outlets and inexplicable valves,
then pulling open the weather-tight, kick-paneled door

and stepping inside, imagining a new life
in which they have traded the brick ranch with large yard
for something that fits into their garage, something
that promises the wide world in its narrow windows.

Is it normal to be transfixed by their hunger for travel,
their zeal for adventure, albeit adventure with comforts,
albeit comforts miniaturized and bolted to the floor?
I fall briefly in love with the tall man ducking

head and shoulders into a cupboard compactly built
into a corner, while his skinny wife reaches up
to the ceiling, single-handedly lowers a bed.
She lies down. Is it normal to think that this bed

would be comfortable? It's not as comfortable as
nearly anything, but it is under a TV on a hinged arm,
and so close to the kitchen that you can reach for ice cream
without missing your show, which I appreciate

because *Your New RV* is my show,
with its timeless message that time flies, a message
as familiar and astonishing as the cataract of water
that gushes from the tiny showerhead,

briefly drenching the floor.
The middle-aged couple in Episode Three
want a break from corporate jobs, and the chance
to spend more time with their ten-year old twins,

but is it normal not to know that next year the ten-year-olds
will turn thirteen? In the next episode a white-haired couple
falls in love with a feature that seems to me unremarkable:
if you lift a handle beside the sink you can drop trash

into a garbage can below, behind the RV's front left wheel.
The couple walks outside and opens and closes and opens
the door that reveals the garbage can. Is this normal, such
open delight? Oh, I know that there is no such thing

as normal, not definitively. Normal is up for debate,
like the relative virtues of the tow-behind-car RV
vs. the motor-inclusive model. Most of the RVs
are the tow-behind variety, but I wonder if it's normal

to want to drive your own car all day
and then not want to stay in a hotel with a big bathroom
and gift shops and restaurants. Wouldn't you want
to order room service, eat on a king-size bed?

I study *Your New RV* as if it were a tutorial
on dreams, on desire. At the end of each episode,
when the people reveal which RV they have chosen,
they are wearing fresh clothes, having spent the night

at home, probably as sleepless as I am now.
They stand before two sets of keys, as sooner or later
we all do. I try to guess which RV they will choose.
They choose. Everything seems alright.

MIDGE

Hi. I'm Midge.
Midge. Barbie's best friend.
I rode beside her in the Dream Car
if Ken couldn't be found,
if Barbie didn't speed off alone.

I'm cute, right? And sporty
in my blue coulottes
and red tam, my tennis racket,
while Barbie's sport, mostly,
was dressing up, from *Barbie Barbeque*

to *Solo in the Spotlight*:
white blouse with billowy sleeves,
magenta velvet maxi-skirt
with rhinestone buttons,
a sap-green silk belt.

Solo came with a microphone.
Sometimes, when Barbie was lying
on the bedroom floor,
her sharp little feet peeking out
from under the dust ruffle,

I would take that mike
and I would wail.
I would twist at my waist
and raise both my arms
and I would wail,

the mike my Dream Car,
my sleek pink convertible
with tail fins. Where would it
take me? I never knew.
Not for me the Dream House,

the patent leather carrying case
with its cardboard hangers,
its little jammed drawers
of accessories. Not for me
the hours spent deciding,

Does this go with this?
Does this go with this?
Barbie would ask me,
and what could I say?
I wanted to say,

Barbie, it all goes together.
Not for me the pillbox hats
and poof-toed stilettos.
What could I, Midge, sell to America?
I needed nothing.

If Barbie was happy, I was happy.

ALFREDO GERMONT EATS A GRANOLA BAR

La Traviata, Taconic Opera, April 2021, Depew Park, Peekskill, NY

Alfredo, who can blame you
for, during First Intermission, sitting
in the grass, eating a granola bar?

After meeting the woman you've loved
from afar, holding her as she faints,
mortally ill, in your arms,

who can blame you for courting,
if briefly, the April breeze,
the shower of tiny yellow flutes

the trees drop into our laps?
In your charcoal wool suitcoat
and red cravat, you struggle

to open the cellophane wrapper,
to savor the small treat hidden
by your large, expressive hands,

by the distance imposed on us
by pandemic's slow retreat.
Alfredo, it seems scripted

that you eat a power-snack,
for you know what lies ahead.
You have rehearsed this role

for over one year, in the isolation
of quarantine: you, Violetta,
your father, the nurse, not to mention

six surviving members of the chorus,
each of you singing alone
in your rooms. You, Alfredo,

practiced until you believed
that your love will cure Violetta,
as it never once has.

Masked and frightened, still
we have gathered in the municipal park
at the edge of the soccer field

as if to see this alone, Alfredo:
your awkward kneeling in the grass,
your rising in time for Act II.

GLIMMERGLASS OPERA POWER FAILURE

Gounod's *Romeo and Juliet*, Cooperstown, NY, July 30, 2023

Romeo kneels, lifts the white cloth from Juliet's face
      until only the edge touches her lips,
            lifts the cloth toward his own lips,

his head bowed, his face in full shadow.
      Everything in his world has gone dark,
            so when the theater goes dark

we think this is part of the production,
      until footsteps break dead silence, someone
            at stage right announces light will return

in five to ten minutes. So there in the dark we all sit,
      those of us who always expect the worst
            and those of us who always expect the best,

and probably some few of us well-rehearsed
      in life's surprises, who have mastered the art
            of living in the moment. Romeo and Juliet

hold steady, one dark figure against ambient light.
      Then, yes, Romeo
            takes the hand of his love,

who is still reclining. He helps her to sit.
      There is some business of adjusting her gown,
            then together they walk off stage.

Why can some imagine a happy ending
      while others fill with dread? How many of us
            discover we welcome

this commodious darkness
      where there is no choice but to wonder
            how one ever goes on?

MARILYN MONROE'S BODY-DOUBLE SPEAKS TO MARILYN'S FANS

Evelyn Moriarty, 1926–2008

Enough! In the time you spend studying Marilyn
you could live your own life. Believe me, I understand
what it is to live through someone else, but that was my job

and I was good at it, proud of my ability to hit my mark,
to stand in Marilyn's size-seven stilettos,
undaunted by the four-inch heels. I came to set costumed

and made-up, ready, if need be, to slip into Marilyn's role,
to impersonate her brilliant impersonation
as if slipping into a pool, to swim long slow laps

inside of my head as the scene played out around me.
That was me you have seen from the back and in the distance,
me walking along the beach while Marilyn lay, again,

in bed, curtains drawn, phone off the hook,
when the doorbell failed to rouse her
a florist leaving on her verandah twelve Mexican lime trees.

Enough, she might have said, turning back into her final sleep,
missing her cue one last time. My sister,
my twin sister, star, diva, pet, famously bad

at memorizing lines which I knew by heart
and still know today. These forty years later,
when finally I speak of her, when I turn my face fully

toward you, see how time has touched me.
Like a lover, time has run its fingers along my cheeks.
It has traced my jawline, cupped my chin.

This is the face that Marilyn would have had,
had she lived, had she been here to say to you the lines
that now I speak: Your life is enough. Any life is enough.

POEM FOR R. K.

I'm in some hotel room tossing clothes
into an open suitcase as if I'm a starlet
in a 1930s movie, just told she has ten minutes
to make the last train out of town.

I close the suitcase. One sleeve hangs out.
I close it again. Then I realize I have nothing
to wear, save for one dress on the floor,
wrinkled as spinach. I drop it over my head.

I slide the suitcase *thunk* to the floor.
I grip its handle and lift, my heart pounding
so hard that it wakes me from this dream
I've had for 30 years, but only this morning

do I understand that this dream is my penance
for leaving you waiting for me
on the southeast corner of campus, at the top
of the stony hill everyone called The Cow Path.

You stood there, I'm sure of it, as we'd agreed,
noon. You shaded your eyes as you looked for me,
not yet understanding I would never appear.
It was a Friday, small groups of students

walking past you as they headed into town
for a last beer of the semester. Your bags were packed,
and mine. You kicked at the dirt, loosening pebbles.
You looked at your watch. I imagine you waited

half an hour, then ten minutes more. You began
to worry. Had I fallen? Had I discovered
that my bag was too heavy and started over,
selecting only the essentials for our life together?

Ron, I imagine your rare anger came to you
slowly, mixing into the sadness, as slowly
as I see that, these years later, you may not remember
that day at all, or you may remember standing there

but have forgotten why. But in case something
inside of you remembers, I want you to know
that I am still waiting to understand why I left you there,
or anywhere, and why, almost every night, I remember.

LITERARY DISCUSSION

We're standing in the conference room, discussing
Emily Dickinson's scientific eye, when at some point
I say *Angie*, as in Angie Dickinson, and I stop dead,

blanch, fake-cough, start to back away,
when I notice no one seems to have heard me say *Angie*.
They probably are too young to remember her,

she of the lacquered white-blond pageboy that never moved
from the early sixties until maybe today, for I think
she is still alive, and so I let my slip slide, sure as Angie

performing a soft-shoe beside Frank Sinatra, both of them
wearing tuxedos but Angie wearing only the top half,
her long legs bare except for glossy nylon stockings,

Angie of the turquoise eyeshadow, her eyes, whatever
she trained them upon, full of adoration, as a poet's eyes
must be, I believe. I could probably relate this to Emily,

whose love for the world was thwarted by the world
yet never dimmed, witness the scrapbooks she assembled
of wildflowers and grasses accompanied by Latin names

in her tiny script. As the discussion continues,
I cannot help but hear Angie's soft purr of a voice
and my father's newspaper crinkling in his lap

when he heard Angie and looked up at the TV,
at the only woman he'd ever found beautiful
except for my mother. The show was *Police Woman*,

which aired from 1974 to 1978, approximately
the worst years of my life. Angie was Pepper Anderson,
an undercover cop in L.A. With a bit of sleuthing,

I discover that, as of 2023, *Police Woman is the oldest
live action television series with all of its main actors
still living, including nonagenarian Dickinson and Earl Holliman.*

Wasn't Holliman involved in Watergate? No,
   that was Halderman,
and a different world from the one in which we now live,
or maybe it's the same world but with different actors.

My father's been dead nearly 15 years, my mother
two months later. I read on Wikipedia that *By the last season
of Police Woman, Dickinson tired of appearing in scenes*

'where the phone rings while I'm taking a bath.' Don't we all?
I mean, is there any one of us who is not awash with the time
in which we live, in which we have lived?

Did you know that Emily Dickinson loved to bake?
I offer. *She was famous for her bread and cakes.*
What feeds us? I wonder. I mean, why do we stand together

and talk poetry as if we understand where it comes from,
as if it isn't nearly always a surprise, and almost embarrassing
how much we love it?

WALT WHITMAN PHOTOGRAPH WITH
THE BUTTERFLY ON HIS FINGER

Walt Whitman Homestead, August 2019

How lucky is this, to be in a room full of people
who have spent their lives loving Walt Whitman,
studying the famous photograph where the poet poses

with a butterfly on his finger? They agree
that the butterfly is cardboard, cut from an Easter card
with glittering script on each wing, *Immortal Life.*

It was manufactured by the hundreds, hundreds lost,
but they cannot agree when this photograph first appeared,
perhaps circa 1940, in a suitcase of yellowed papers

before which a woman yawped in the form of a gasp.
Could Whitman himself ever have been more delighted
than she, who knelt in her parents' attic

under the eaves of her childhood home,
she who is suddenly unsure of her age,
if anyone would miss her if she stayed here forever?

This is a question that the scholars cannot answer,
but they agree that the butterfly casts a spell
on whoever looks upon it, and thus they return

to the subject at hand: Whitman sits, in profile,
his long beard a slash of white light
between dark hat and black suitcoat,

uniform the poet adopted in early middle age,
when he still looked like the young man
on the frontispiece of the first edition of *Leaves of Grass*:

arms akimbo in loose shirt with suspenders,
sun-bleached hair, for all we know hauling
buckets of water as a breathless artist trails,

begging him to pause for his portrait.
If we are to believe the poems, Whitman was in love
with the grass and with all that walked upon it,

including one man in particular, which is why
friends told the poet to grow his graying beard,
to wear his shirt fully buttoned and under a vest,

the garb of a proper grandfather.
This was his costume for the rest of his life,
from the late nights of wild youth

to the much later nights when he slept in a chair
so as not to wake breathless, gasping for air.
The *butterfly photograph*, as the cognescenti say,

was Whitman's favorite picture of himself:
left hand in jacket pocket, right hand raised
as if giving directions, pointing at something unseen

with the finger on which perches the butterfly
nearly too small for notice except that Walt Whitman
stares at it: a bright blur, like beating wings,

like a tear in fabric, through which light pours.

AT THE FEET OF MICHELANGELO'S *DAVID*

They are not the first couple to stand at the feet of *David*
and kiss as if they are saying goodbye at a train station

with one suitcase set between them and the conductor
leaning out his window, bringing the whistle

to his mouth but not yet blowing it,
pressing the cool metal to his lower lip as he watches

travelers rush past the couple as water rushes
around a stone in a river, oh, like attention itself:

a tumbling, ungovernable thing for all but the geniuses
among us, who somehow can concentrate on something

the tour guide is saying about Michelangelo's study of cadavers.
She wants us to look at David's right hand, which hangs

by his side, slightly oversize, its bulging veins proving
that this is the hand of a living man, pulsing with blood.

It is warm and pliant as the hands of this couple
who stand at the feet of the masterpiece,

who are not the first couple to kiss here, but are the last
for today, for the *Accademia* closes in ten minutes. People

press past to buy postcards, posters, tote bags, to reclaim
their umbrellas, for today in Florence

it is pouring wide angel-wings of rain,
which drips onto the tile floor from the hair

of the couple, from the hems of their coats.
They have come here to get out of the rain.

They kiss at the feet of David because he stands
in the gallery off the lobby, and why should they wait?

What better way to make use of their time, so close
to marble made flesh, to the vast head tilted downward, watching?

THE MUSIC

You've got to face the music, Sweetie, my father would say,
this refrain of my childhood chiming surer than Sunday's
church bells, than the neighbor's pug barking at every car.

He'd say it, and then say nothing else, as if he trusted
that I already understood this, my first metaphor. He knew
that time would soon enough teach me the music

of the broken arm, the weak eye, the eyepatch,
the music of swimming lessons in the cold lake,
my teeth chattering as dark fish pin-wheeled against my legs.

Already there had been the music of screeching tires
and the final yelp of Jill Ruben's beagle, Jill sobbing
on her porch, pausing only to call her dog's name.

Already there must have been the music of a small lump
in my grandmother's breast, years before the bed
in the living room, the silver tree with ten-dollar bills

clothes-pinned to it, sent by her friends at the factory.
There must have been the music of the first cell
missing its cue in my mother's brain, adding a beat

to the time it took her to recognize us. Already
I had seen TV news: helicopters like quarter-notes
lifting from jungles, palm trees shredding in updraft,

years before I knew the acapella of second-hand sorrow,
the strained harmony of making a living
from a steady job that works you into the ground.

This was years before I had to face the music of time passing,
face that, without time, there could be no music at all—
no Mozart, no Motown, no voice of the one you most love, leaning
    close.

There could be no labored music of the high school band
in which the deaf boy plays the triangle,
thanks to the conductor's deep and timely nod,

nor the music of the boy's face as he strikes his note,
nor as he places his hand on the shivering silver
to cue the inevitable silence.

Now I think that, with his silence, my father
was teaching me the music of silence, and to face it, too,
as if with the deaf boy's stubborn love

for what he cannot hear, which sings to him
as if he were its brother, its son,
as if he were its father.

RODEO

for Scott Wheeler

There are better ways to do this,
        but I listen to Copland's ballet on a car radio
                in the foothills of the Catskills, driving

the long way home for no reason I know
        other than to see gold leaves,
                old orchards, and horse farms,

weekend homes of the wealthy
        who drive up from Manhattan
                Friday night, and head back Monday

at sunrise, which is this movement:
        violins like footsteps across grass,
                violas and cellos poised to follow,
to reach and sway like something stretching awake.
        The composer conjures morning
                when I most need morning,

late afternoon in early November.
        The two-lane road winds in and out
                of the music, which,

when I cannot hear it, seems gone entirely
        before it rises again, weaving through a broadcast
                from another station, on which listeners

argue about a quarterback benched for a penalty.
        They debate the referee's call, so loudly
                it seems that they, too, hear *Rodeo*

building to crescendo, so they raise their voices
        before the hills absorb them,
                as the hills will absorb each of us,

eventually. It is hard not to think of my dead.
        It is hard to believe that, around the next curve,
                the music will resume not where it left off,

but from where it never left off,
        from where it keeps playing, inside
                this cold earth, its late fruits,

MacIntosh and Granny Smith and Rome
        in crates at the side of the road,
                free for the taking.

CREDITS

I thank the editors of the following publications, in which my poems, sometimes in earlier versions, first appeared:

American Journal of Poetry.com: "What You Get"

Asheville Poetry Review: "Again, I Hear Myself Lecturing My Students on a Subject About Which I Know Very Little" and "Sophia Loren Reveals Her Secret to Staying Young"

Braving the Body: "Emergency Room"

Comstock Review: "Lovespoon"

The Forward Book of Poetry 2022: "For the Poet Who Writes to Me While Standing in Line at CVS, Waiting for His Mother's Prescription"

The Helix Literary Magazine: "The Music," as 2023 Leslie McGrath Poetry Prize, Runner-up

I Wanna Be Loved By You: Poems on Marilyn Monroe (Milk and Cake Press, Cincinnati, Ohio, 2022): "Marilyn Monroe's Body-Double Speaks to Marilyn's Fans"

The Irish Times: "For the Poet Who Writes to Me While Standing in Line…"

Lightwood: "To the Person at the Zoom Poetry Reading, Unmuted, Doing Hand Laundry"

Limpwristmagazine.com (Barbie Issue): "Midge"

The Manhattan Review: "The War," "I Think I've Figured It All Out,"and "The Beauty"

The Moth: "For the Poet Who Writes to Me While Standing in Line…"

New Ohio Review: "Brief Guide," "Cahoots," and "Who Among Us"

Paterson Literary Review: "Hermina" and "Is It Normal?"

Poetry International (online): "Alfredo Germont Eats a Granola Bar"

Southern Review: "It is Said"

Southern Poetry Review: "Worry Stone"

Southword 46: New International Writing: "At the Feet of Michelangelo's *David,*" as Gregory O'Donoghue International Poetry Prize Winner, 2nd Place, selected by Mary O'Donnell

"For the Poet Who Writes to Me While Standing in Line at CVS, Waiting for His Mother's Prescription" was selected by Nick Laird as one of four poems shortlisted for the 2020 Moth Poetry Prize.

"In Memory of the Forgotten" was selected as a finalist for The Watchword Prize, judged by Carolyn Forche, and featured in the November 2024 conference "The Color of Surveillance: Surveillance/Resistance" hosted by the Center on Privacy and Technology at Georgetown Law.

THANKS

I thank my beloved, talented, patient, and generous first-readers: Mara Bergman, Carl Dennis, Al Maginnes, Dana Roeser, and Richard Tillinghast. I thank my Writing Friends group: Nadine Ellsworth-Moran, Zorina Frey, Lisa Hase-Jackson, and Susan Tekulve.

For my three poetry angels—Ellen Bass, Jan Beatty, and Dorianne Laux—I am grateful beyond words for your poetry and your support of mine. For the Converse University MFA in Creative Writing Program, both colleagues and students: I learn from each of you, with joy.

I thank the Laura Boss Poetry Foundation for sponsoring the Laura Boss Narrative Poetry Award and thank Jan Beatty for selecting my manuscript. I thank the Foundation for selecting as publisher NYQ Books. I feel I have won the jackpot.

I thank Raymond P. Hammond for his extensive and gracious expertise in the production of this book.

David, without you it's all just words.

ABOUT THE AUTHOR

Suzanne Cleary is the author of four books of poetry, most recently *Crude Angel* (2018). *Beauty Mark* was chosen by Kevin Prufer as winner of the 2012 John Ciardi Prize. Her chapbook *Blue Cloth* was chosen by Marilyn Nelson and Robert Cording as winner of the Sunken Garden Poetry Prize. Recipient of a Pushcart Prize, her other awards include fellowships from the New York Foundation for the Arts, Yaddo, MacDowell, and the Cecil Hemley Memorial Award of the Poetry Society of America. Her poems appear in anthologies including *Best American Poetry* and in journals including *The Atlantic*, *Poetry*, *Southern Review*, *Manhattan Review*, *Poetry International*, and *Poetry London*. She is Core Faculty in the MFA in Creative Writing Program of Converse University.

suzanneclearypoet.com

www.ingramcontent.com/pod-product-compliance
Lightning Source LLC
Chambersburg PA
CBHW022014080426
42733CB00007B/596